Joint Smoking Rules

by
Simon Worman

Illustrated by **Carmen Cerra**

(Based on original illustrations by **Mike Hageman)**

THE TELEGRAPH COMPANY
BROOKLYN, NEW YORK
PITTSBURGH, PENNSYLVANIA

ORIGINAL, UNOFFICIAL JOINT SMOKING RULES ©2001 by Simon Worman. All rights reserved. Printed in the United States of America. No part of this book may be used or reproduced in any manner whatsoever without written permission except in the case of brief quotations embodied in critical articles and reviews. For information contact The Telegraph Company at 330 Brownsville Rd, First Floor, Pittsburgh, PA 15210, or via email, info@thetelegraphcompany.com.

Design by Daniel Shepelavy

LCCN 2001088629

Forward

I've been burning joints as long as there have been matches! Or does it just seem that long? I may have only started yesterday! So confused...

Oh well! Anyway, throughout the years, we've come across a lotta joint smoking rules. One day, we decided to write these rules down and explain them. I'm pretty sure these are the:

Original, Un-Official Joint Smoking Rules

And remember:
There is an exception to every rule!

Thank You!

I would like to thank everyone who has been a part of this book. From the people who have come up with rules, to those who have broken them. And to all who have given me inspiration and motivation to turn our rules into a book. Especially my friend Mac, who truly helped make these rules a reality. But most of all, I'd like to thank Kaye, for helping me make this really special. And let's not forget A.J.! Last, but not least, All Three Mikes. Did you think I would forget any of you?!?!

And More Thank Yous:
Since the first printing of this book, I've met a lot of cool people. I'd like to thank them all especially THE PHIL ZONE (Lawrence, KS) and IT'S A BEAUTIFUL DAY (KC, MO) the stores that sold the book from the beginning because they too believed in it. Also, Jack Margolis, Tommy Chong, Cheech Marin, Mojo Nixon, Bob Marley, Peter Tosh, N.O.R.M.L., Kai, Kurt H enning, The Note, Alternative Index Magazine, Patric Quinn, Madonna, Sound, KJHK, KKFI, Scooter and his friend Bob, and everyone else I've forgotten to mention.

Author's Note

This is a book of humor.

I don't need to explain why I wrote it.

If you don't smoke marijuana, yet have a healthy sense of humor, then you'll have a good laugh.

If you don't condone the smoking of marijuana, I respect your opinion. All I ask is that you respect my First Amendment right to free speech.

I'm not selling drugs, only humor.

The Have Some Stash Rule:
(remember, no bunkweed!)

This rule says it all: if you don't have any marijuana, you can't smoke a joint.

If you don't have a joint, this book won't mean a whole lot to you.

If you do have a joint, Simon Sez: Spark it up!

The Rolling Paper Rule: Without rolling papers, you cannot roll a joint.

This rule is as important as the first rule. Try and remember this: if you need rolling papers after partaking in a joint, DO NOT go to the 7-11 to buy them. They aren't sold there and it only makes the person behind the counter look at you as if you were an alien.

NOTE: *If you're as clever as my buddy Kai, then you will always have one stashed here for emergencies.*

Emergency Paper Stash

The Fire Rule:
You must have some fire to light the joint.

Otherwise, you can't smoke it.

Matches, a lighter, even a magnifying glass in direct sunlight will work. However, rubbing two sticks together is not real effective in this situation.

The Stashing the Pot When Authority Figures Arrive Rule.

If the Authorities show up at your door, it is EVERYBODY's responsibility to look for anything that could be considered contraband and hide it.

The penalty for breaking this rule could be a long stay in the City, County or State Hotel. So, please, do not break this rule.

NOTE: *This rule was moved up due to the important nature of this subject.*

The Not Cleaning the Stash Rule.

This rule covers both rolling a joint with a seed in it and/or rolling a joint with a stem in it.

You must always be sure that your stash is clean before rolling a joint. If a seed explodes in a bearded person's face due to the fact that you did not clean the stash properly, you could be **severely beaten.**

The second part of this rule is not as severe as the first. Sometimes a joint will smoke with a stem in it. In this case, you got lucky and will not be penalized.

Remember, to clean the stash properly, be sure to use the "Braille" method of feeling the weed and making sure that it's clean!

The Lighting The Joint Properly Rule.

This rule is very important, because you always want to ensure that your joints don't run.

It is not the fault of the joint roller if the joint runs due to improper lighting technique.

The proper lighting procedure is as follows: Inhale with the flame touching the joint. Don't light the joint away from your mouth. Lighting a joint on fire and then bringing it to your mouth to inhale is a punishable offense.

The "If You Wanna Smoke One" Rule.

Basically, this rule says that if you want to smoke a joint, you have to be able to roll one.

Paper surrounding stash does **not** constitute a rolled joint. The joint should be cylindrical and the stash evenly distributed across the length of the paper. Nor should it look like a piece of candy, all twisted at the ends!

NOTE: *Some people get out of this job by supplying stash for someone else to roll. This is an acceptable exception to the rule.*

Another **NOTE:** *Just because I roll a perfect joint* (see Rule #59) *does not mean I'm going to give away my secrets. This means I'm not going to tell everyone how to do it!*

The Rolling a Joint With a Hole In It Rule.

While always considered poor form, sometimes violating this rule carries no penalty. If the hole is small enough, and you can put your finger over it and use the hole as a carburetor until you've burned past it, then it will be o.k.

If the hole is so big that this is not possible and you must re-roll it, then you have also broken the **Re-rolling a Joint Rule** *(see Rule #13).*

The Rolling a Joint Too Small Rule.

Hopefully, everyone is intelligent enough not to break this rule.

We must assume that the only possible reason why this rule would be broken is due to insufficient amounts of stash.

If you're out of stash, you are allowed to roll a small joint. If that's the case, then you are in accordance with **The Last Hooter Rule** *(see Rule #75).*

We can't give you an exact measure as to the amount of stash that is in a proper joint. This is as subjective and territorial as how you choose your favorite nickname for marijuana. However, weight should be approximately 0.5-0.7 grams.

The Don't Argue With The Roller Rule.

You must always remember this rule. The penalty for breaking this rule could be the entire joint.

If the roller is also the owner of the stash, you could also be breaking the **Insulting the Owner of the Stash Rule** *(see Rule #33).*

The penalty for breaking one or both of these rules extends for the entire length of your visit. This means that you are cut off!

NOTE: *If you break both of these rules, make sure that the roller/owner is not your connection. If this is the case, you could be bummin'.*

The If You Rolled It Rule.

This is another simple rule. If you rolled the joint, then you **definitely** have to help smoke it.

NOTE: *There are no exceptions to this rule.*

The Rolling A Joint That Won't Smoke Rule.

If you roll a joint that won't smoke, you must re-roll the joint. The penalty is that you are not allowed to partake of the re-rolled joint.

NOTE: *We understand that this is a stiff penalty, but if you want to smoke a joint, you should at least be able to roll one* (see Rule #7).

ANOTHER NOTE: *It has been brought to our attention that there are joints that will smoke, but will not smoke in a Power Hitter™. Power Hitters™ are classified as luxury items, or extras, which not all of us are fortunate enough to have. Therefore, while it is still a punishable offense to roll a joint that won't smoke in one, it does not warrant a separate rule.*

ONE MORE NOTE: *You might be able to avoid the penalty by complying with the **Re-rolling the Joint Rule*** (see Rule #13).

The Re-Rolling the Joint Rule.

If the joint has to be re-rolled, you have one more chance to try (and succeed).

Should you fail this time, the joint will be rolled by someone else. The joint will be bigger and you will not be allowed to smoke any of it. Even if it's rolled from your stash.

NOTE: *In the event that it is your stash and you get pissed off and proceed to leave with said stash, you are then breaking the **Asshole Rule** (see Rule #42).*

The Newspaper Rule.

A 1 1⁄4 width rolling paper is more than sufficient to roll a joint. Most people prefer to smoke marijuana, not paper.

If you're using enough paper to write on, then you should be a journalist. Make up your mind: Are you rolling a joint or writing a book?

The Roll A Joint First Rule.

If you have a roommate and there is enough stash on the tray, you should be polite and have a joint rolled and ready for his or her arrival home.

This not only allows your roommate to relax, but it strengthens the bond of friendship as well.

If you live with more than one roommate, it is very likely that one of them will be caught by the **You Snooze You Lose Rule** *(see Rule #31).*

The Bogart Rule.

Don't take more than the toke you're allowed.
Going through life with a nickname like
Humphrey or Hoover could be psychologically
and emotionally damaging.

The penalty for breaking this rule is at least one
toke for each time the rule is broken. If you
continue to break this rule, stiffer penalties can
and, most likely, **will** be enforced.

NOTE: *We have discovered that breaking this
rule in some places could be fatal.*

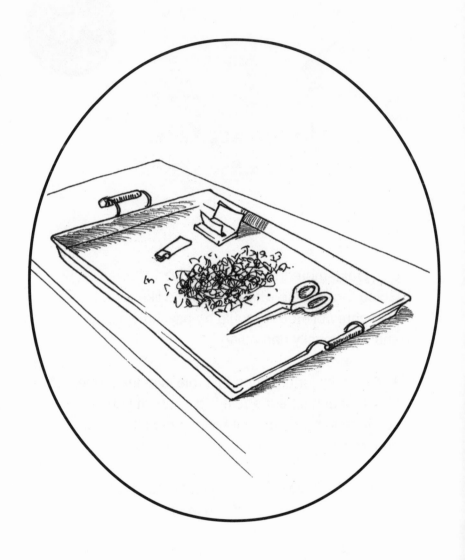

The On The Tray Rule.

If the tray is left out, and there is pot on it, feel free to help yourself! That is what it's there for.

After all, marijuana is meant to be shared.

The Air Freshener Rule.

Don't let the joint burn without someone taking a hit.

The penalty for breaking this rule depends upon the availability of stash. You could be severely beaten for wasting precious smoke. How much punishment is exacted depends on how close your friends really are.

The Don't Let The Joint Run Rule.

When a joint comes to you and it is running, don't be an asshole: fix it!

First, turn the joint up so that the side with the run is on top (heat rises, remember). Proceed to take smooth, slow tokes, thus allowing the hot air to rise and create a fire along the paper that needs to be burn away. Next, wet your index finger (ladies, please be careful of your nails) and make a complete circle around the joint, starting at the lowest burning point.

If you break this rule, you might get away with blaming it on the person who had the joint before you. This depends on how badly the joint is running.

NOTE: *If you're smoking a joint that I rolled, you won't have this problem because my joints never run. See the **Rolling a Perfect Joint Rule** (Rule #59).*

OFFICIAL RULE NO. 20

The In The Middle Rule.

This is one of my personal favorites. If you're in the middle and you have to keep passing the joint back and forth, you are allowed to double toke the joint. Trafficking fees, of course.

You don't have to double toke, but you are allowed to do so. As long as you are in the middle, you cannot be penalized under the **Bogart Rule** *(see Rule #16)*.

Unless, of course, you get caught breaking the **In The Middle Bogart Rule** *(see Rule #21)*.

NOTE: *This rule is limited to three person situations. When there are more than three people, double toking is in violation of the* **Bogart Rule** (see rule #16).

The In The Middle Bogart Rule.

As with Rule #20, this rule is limited to three person situations. If you are in the middle, you are allowed to double toke, but you are not allowed to keep toking and toking while you space out. This is the point at which you cross the line.

The penalty for breaking this rule is the same as the **Bogart Rule** *(see Rule #16).*

The Burn One With Your Supplier Rule.

When you score some smoke, be sure to say "thank you" to your connection by smoking a joint together.

Sometimes, due to time constraints or other circumstances, this may not be possible. In this instance, please leave enough of your stash for a future joint with them. Don't be stingy; without your connection, you wouldn't have a stash to enjoy. And you might not see the humor of this book.

NOTE: *The penalty for this is the possibility of losing your connection and that is hitting you where it hurts, you know what I mean?*

The Letting The Joint Go Out Rule.

If you can't pay attention to a lit object in your hand, then you don't need to be smoking a joint.

You must watch out for people who break this rule. These people should be cut off indefinitely.

The Giving a Joint To The Person Who Is Already Penalized Rule.

If you give the joint to someone who is already penalized for breaking a rule, then you become the penalized person and the original rule breaker is exonerated of his/her wrongdoings.

NOTE: *Beware of people who are penalized and try to catch you with this rule.*

The Lightweight Rule.
(a.k.a. The Weak Tit Rule.)

If you're too wimpy to smoke the joint that is currently being passed around, they you're obviously too wimpy to smoke another and, therefore, are not allowed to smoke for the rest of your visit.

NOTE: *You are shit-out-of-luck if you Lightweight-out during the first or second joint of the day. Aren't you Donny?*

The Vintage Rule.

This rule is the only rule that allows you to Lightweight-out without breaking the **Lightweight Rule** *(see Rule #25).*

In order to claim the Vintage Rule, you must be the oldest person in the room.

NOTE: *I would like to thank our buddy, "Old Shortcut" for bringing this rule to my attention.*

The Last Joint of the Night Rule.

Everyone has to smoke the last joint of the night before going to bed or leaving, whichever the case may be.

The Knocking Over The Tray Rule.

This is also known as the **Death Penalty Rule.**
Especially if what was on the tray was all that
was left.

People usually die in this situation, so please
pay attention and do not break this rule.

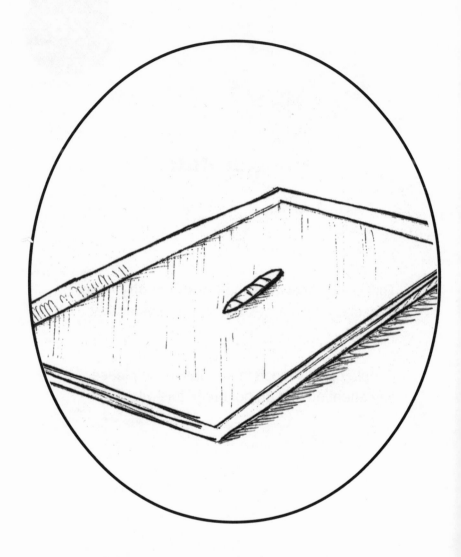

The Smoking The Last Joint On The Tray Rule.

Never smoke the last joint on the tray by yourself.

You must share the last joint on the tray with your roommate. If you have no roommate, you must then share it with a friend.

If you do smoke the last joint on the tray by yourself, then you are also breaking the **Bogart Rule** *(see Rule #16)* and the **Asshole Rule** *(see Rule #42)*. Please share.

The Not Leaving Something On The Tray Rule.

Family does not leave family without leaving something on the tray.

This is cruel and unusual punishment, unless of course you have nothing to leave. In which case, we're all shit-out-of-luck.

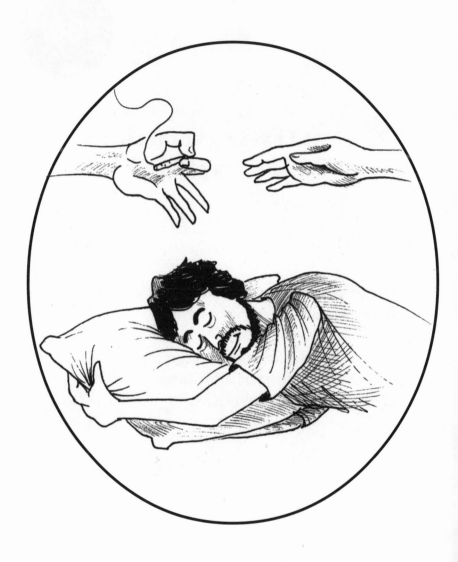

The You Snooze You Lose Rule.

If you aren't around when the joint is burning, it is your loss.

The Taking Longer Than The Allotted Amount Of Time Rule.

If someone has to keep reminding you to take your hit, or you take too long to take your toke, you lose it.

Habitual breakers of this rule will also be breaking the **You Snooze You Lose Rule** *(see Rule #31).*

NOTE: Habitual breakers of Rule #32 could also be subject to penalties under the **Bogart Rule** *(see #16)*

The Insulting The Owner Of The Stash Rule.

You must never insult the owner of the stash. Especially when they are rolling the joint *(see Rule #10).*

If you break this rule, you may be cut off.

The Holding Out Rule.

If someone comes over and they have a joint and don't smoke it with you, they are breaking this rule. If you are breaking this rule, you are also breaking the **Asshole Rule** *(see Rule #42).*

The penalty for this could be severe. We've said it before and we'll say it again: Marijuana was meant to be shared. If you have a joint, you should share it.

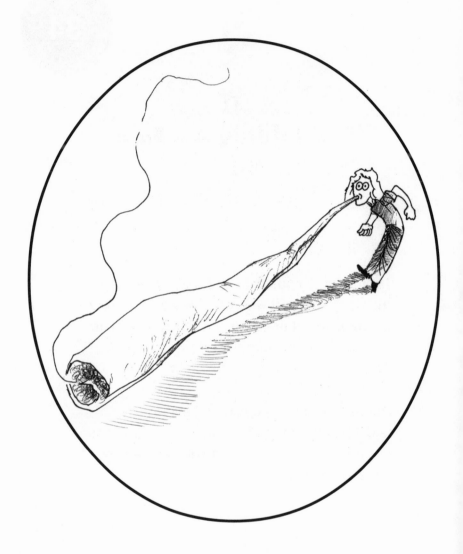

The Endless Joint Rule.

No matter how long a joint seems to burn, you must smoke it until it's all gone.

In the event that this is your last joint, you may save some of it.

The Changing Or Forgetting Direction Rule.

This is a treacherous rule. The more joints you smoke, the more often this rule is broken, so please be aware.

It is important to remember where the joint came from and which way it is going. Individuals in the middle are prone to breaking this rule, and can sometimes keep from being penalized by invoking the **In The Middle Rule** *(see Rule #20).* However, if they cross the line, they are breaking the **In The Middle Bogart Rule** *(see Rule #21).*

The Turn-About Rule.

If someone calls your name more than three times to take a joint, and you still don't take it, then the joint does a turn-about and starts to travel in the other direction. You then become the end of the line.

When breaking this rule, you not only lose the joint for yourself, but you could piss off the person next to you who **was** paying attention. This could result in bodily harm.

NOTE: *Just ask Taylor.*

The Changing Place In Line Rule.

Every so often, you will encounter a person who moves back and forth in line to get extra tokes. This usually happens in large groups of people.

At times this is purely coincidental. There are even times when it is accidental. Regardless, you are still breaking a rule, so watch yourself!

The penalty could be severe, especially if you are caught repeatedly breaking this rule.

OFFICIAL
39
RULE NO.

The When You Get Caught With Two Joints At The Same Time Rule.

When you're at a party, or there just happens to be two or more joints going in different directions at the same time, and they both end up in your hands, you must definitely take a hit off both joints. Trafficking fees, of course.

If both joints are going in the same direction, and they both end up in your hands, then you are smoking too slowly. In this case you could be breaking the **Taking Longer Than The Allotted Amount Of Time Rule** *(see Rule #32).*

The Hospitality Rule

If a friend comes to your house bearing gifts, you must always say thank you by smoking a joint with them.

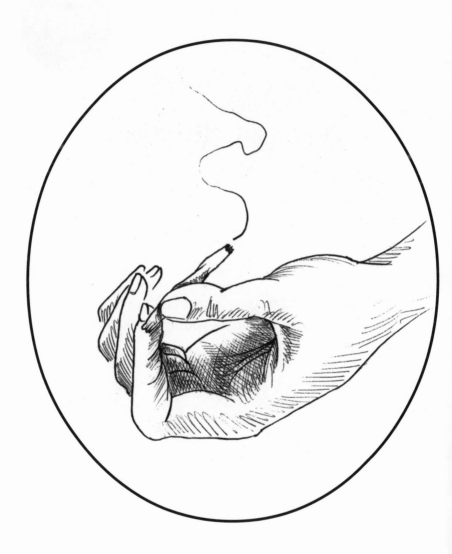

The Proper Way To Pass A Joint Rule.

The proper way to pass a joint is with your hand cupped upward and around the fire and ashes. Should you drop the joint while passing it, it will fall into your hand and not on the floor.

NOTE: *This is definitely the procedure to follow in Kaye's house.*

The Asshole Rule.

This rule is about people who are assholes because they won't let you have a hit even though it's your turn.

Sometimes they play the teasing game, holding the joint just out of your reach. No matter how far you stretch to reach them, they are always just out of reach. These people are assholes and should be totally cut off!

NOTE: *If you break the **Re-Rolling The Joint Rule** (see Rule #13) and get pissed off and leave with the stash you are also breaking the **Asshole Rule.***

ANOTHER NOTE: *If you break the **Smoke The Last Joint On The Tray Rule** (see Rule #29) you are a true asshole and are breaking this rule too.*

YET ANOTHER NOTE: *If you break the **Holding Out Rule** (Rule #34), you are also an asshole and have broken two rules.*

ONE FINAL NOTE: *If you break the **Over-Indulging Rule** (see Rule #43), everyone will tell you what an asshole you are.*

The Over-Indulging Rule.

Over-indulging is when the person in front of you decides they want to take as long and slow a hit as possible, just to make you wait. If this person coughs, they are breaking the **Over Indulging Rule.**

The penalty if you break this rule is that everyone in the room will slap the shit out of you and tell you just what kind of an asshole you really are. However, this is not to be confused with the **Asshole Rule** *(see Rule #42).* And as if that weren't bad enough, you also won't be allowed to partake in at least the rest of this joint, and perhaps the next one as well.

The West Coast Rule.

This rule is applicable in California and the West coast of Florida, and pertains to watching sunsets.

If you go to the beach to watch a sunset, you must always take at least one joint. Failure to do so will probably spoil the sunset.

NOTE: *Sometimes you must break this rule due to the presence of authority figures* (see Rule #4).

The Don't Come Over Without a Joint Rule.

As your mother (hopefully) told you, if you've been invited to someone's house, you should never arrive empty handed. Therefore, if you go to someone's house, be sure to take a joint.

Of course, there will be times when you can't bring a joint because you simply don't have one. This is a valid excuse, unless it becomes a habit, in which case you are breaking the **Coming Over and Mooching Joints Rule** *(see Rule #46)*.

The Coming Over And Mooching Joints Rule.

There are certain people who always seem to be around when you're ready to smoke a joint. It also seems like these people never have a joint. This is very inconsiderate.

The penalty ranges from social isolation to a severe beating.

NOTE: *Thanks to Doc, it has been brought to our attention that individuals guilty of breaking this rule are stricken with "Gots-to-Go" disease. As in: "I've finished the joint and I've gots to go!"*

The Dropping The Joint Rule.

Dropping a joint every once in a while is ok. However, if you hand someone a joint and they consistently (more than three times) drop it, they are breaking the rules.

Once a person breaks this rule, it is obvious that he or she is too stoned to smoke and should be cut off immediately.

Should this happen, the person in question is also breaking the **Too Stoned To Smoke Rule** *(see rule #53).*

The Tossing The Joint Rule.

There are times when passing joints becomes too difficult. At these times, it is easier to toss joints back and forth. When tossed correctly, they are easy to catch and will not burn holes in your carpet.

NOTE: *Some households have very nice carpeting. It is not polite to toss joints in these homes.*

Example: *Toss a joint in Kaye's house and she'll kill you!*

The Don't Get The Joint Wet Rule.

This is simple really: Don't get the joint wet or the damn thing won't smoke!

Sometimes accidents happen and you might drop the joint in a drink. When this happens, you are also breaking the **Dropping a Joint Rule** *(see Rule #47)*.

However, there are other ways to break this rule. If you slobber all over the end of a joint while taking a toke, for example. Your companions may become enraged to discover that you don't understand a simple, basic rule of joint smoking. It is possible that they will no longer allow you to smoke with them.

The Author Of This Book Is Exempt From All Rules Rule.

This is a rule to cover my ass, just in case someday, somewhere, somebody might try to catch me breaking a rule.

NOTE: *This rule applies to Kaye too. However, it should be noted that no one is exempt from the* **Stashing the Pot When Authority Figures Arrive Rule** *(see rule #4).*

The Illustrator Of This Book Is Exempt From All Rules Rule.

Without illustrations, this book wouldn't be nearly as much fun. Therefore, the illustrator is also exempt.

NOTE: *But remember, no one is exempt from the* **Stashing the Pot When Authority Figures Arrive Rule** (see rule #4).

The Smoke The Joint Or Else Rule.

You must either smoke the joint or suffer the owner of the stash's wrath. Refusing hospitality is the height of bad manners.

Note: This rule does not apply to fellow partiers who do not smoke pot.

The Too Stoned To Smoke Rule.

If you're too stoned to smoke the joint being passed around, that is ok. You don't have to smoke any of it.

Just remember, you won't be allowed to smoke any of the next one either.

The New Person
Arriving Rule.

Whenever a person comes to your house, you should smoke a joint together. If you have just finished smoking a joint, you may be exempt by claiming the **You Snooze You Lose Rule** *(see rule #31).*

If a new person is to arrive, you must make sure that they are not breaking the **Don't Come Over Without a Joint Rule** *(see rule #45).* If they aren't breaking the rule, you will get to smoke another joint anyway.

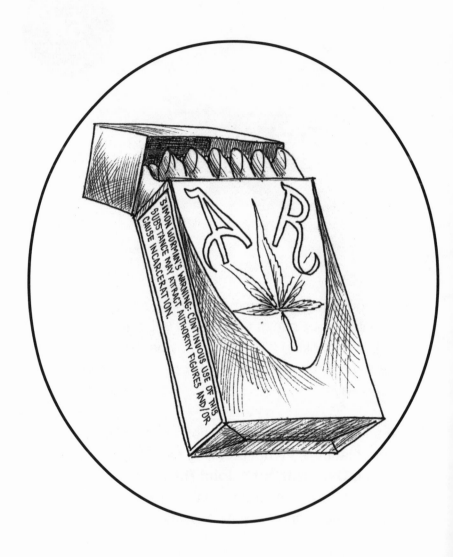

The A-R (Already Rolled) Rule.

If you're going to take a joint somewhere, it's better if it's already rolled (a-r). This makes it easier to smoke while you're out and about. Because, as you probably know, it's hard to roll a joint in the wind!

NOTE: *It has been brought to my attention that these are also called "traveling joints." A traveling joint should have the bottom end folded like an envelope, or be twisted, so that you don't lose stash while traveling.*

OFFICIAL
56
RULE NO.

The Bar Rule.

If you are going to your favorite bar, you must have a bar joint *(similar in concept to the a-r joint, see Rule #55)* ready to smoke with your friends.

If you don't have one to share with them, they may use you as a pool cue in the next bar fight.

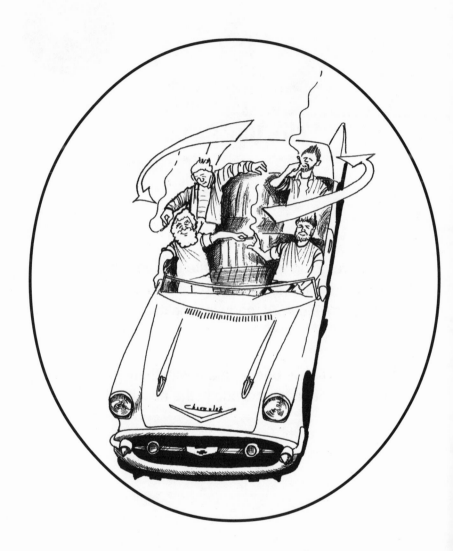

The Cruisin' Rule.

When smoking a joint en route, the direction of the joint should always be counter-clockwise. This means the person in the passenger seat should hand the driver the joint and the driver should pass it behind him and so on.

We must remember not to be obvious about smoking a joint while cruisin'.

Do not take a toke when you are passing, or if you are being passed by, another vehicle. An authority figure could very well be inside.

The Road Trip Rule.

When on a road trip, particularly if it's to get concert tickets or go to a concert, you must smoke continuously. And especially if you're going to see a jam band (I used to say a Grateful Dead show, but as we all know, they're not around anymore).

Remember, the Cruisin' Rule (see rule #57) is always in effect.

NOTE: *When traveling, remain aware of the* ***Border Rule:*** *you must smoke a joint whenever you cross a state line.*

The Rolling The Perfect Joint Rule.

Rolling a perfect joint excludes you from any penalty, especially if it's your stash.

NOTE: *A perfect joint is hand-rolled, not with a rolling machine, but looks as though it were. A perfect joint will never run.*

ANOTHER NOTE: *Practice makes perfect, so practice every day!*

OFFICIAL RULE NO. 60

The Ripping The Last Paper Rule.

If you rip the last paper, you are automatically elected to go to the store and buy some more.

Please refer to the **Rolling Paper Rule** *(see rule #2)* when you run this errand.

The Time To Take A Toke Rule.

All you have to do is say what time it is, and that's the time to take a toke. This rule applies, no matter what time it is.

Example: *"It's 10:37, time to take a toke!"*

NOTE: *This rule existed long before 4:20 did.*

The Bag Delivery Rule.

If you have to deliver a bag of stash, you definitely get to smoke a joint out of it.

The Taking Too Long To Roll A Joint Rule.

There is no exact time limit on rolling a joint. However, it you seem to take forever and day to roll a joint, then you are breaking the rule.

A time limit can be voted on by a show of hands.

NOTE: *It's not a good idea to keep people who really want to smoke a joint waiting.*

If You Bummed A Joint, You Must Roll It Rule.

Bummed joints should be on the small side—it doesn't have to be a pinner, but don't make it a hog leg either. Remember, you are smoking thanks to the generosity of a friend and it's free. So be cool!

NOTE: *If it is necessary to bum a paper to roll with as well, you must smoke said joint with the person who gave up the paper.*

OFFICIAL
RULE NO.
65

The Taking Too Long To Roll The Joint You Just Bummed Rule.

When you've bummed a joint, it's important to keep this in mind: You have just bummed someone's stash, so don't waste their time taking too long to roll the joint.

In the event that you just dropped in to bum a joint, you should make a special effort not to break this rule. However, if you have bummed the joint after partying with the owner(s) of the stash, then leniency is given as everyone is probably high and therefore not as likely to notice the time passing.

The Hospital Rule.

When visiting a friend in the hospital, you must always bring your friend at least one joint.

The Ash Rule.

You must remember to be polite and use an ashtray.

If you let the ash fall on the floor, you could be severely punished. Particularly if your host or hostess has nice carpet.

You are also breaking this rule if you pass a joint with a flickable ash and you're the one closest to the ashtray and don't flick.

The penalty for this is that you must follow the joint around with an ashtray in hand to make sure nobody else breaks this rule.

The Breakfast Joint Rule.

Good morning, it's wake-n-bake time! You must always smoke a breakfast joint, since the first joint of the day is usually the best joint of the day.

NOTE: *You could ruin the entire day if you break this rule and go without.*

The Bedroom Hooter Rule.

If you're heading to your bedroom with a friend, then you definitely need to take a joint with you.

Smoking a joint between passionate lovemaking sessions is wonderful.

NOTE: *If you take a joint to bed, just to smoke one by yourself before you go to sleep, and you neglect everyone else in the house, you are breaking the **Last Joint of The Night Rule*** (see Rule #27).

The After Dinner Joint Rule.

If you are the first to finish the meal, you must roll the after-dinner joint.

Everyone knows a joint tastes especially good after eating.

The Lunch Joint Rule.

Since you probably only have half an hour for lunch, you must hurry to smoke this one because you'll need to eat in this time as well.

Due to the time shortage, your lunch joint must be an a-r *(see rule #55)*.

The Special Occasion Rule.

If you are going somewhere for a special occasion, you need to take along at least one joint.

Example: It's Mike's birthday! I'm going to take him a big fat joint.

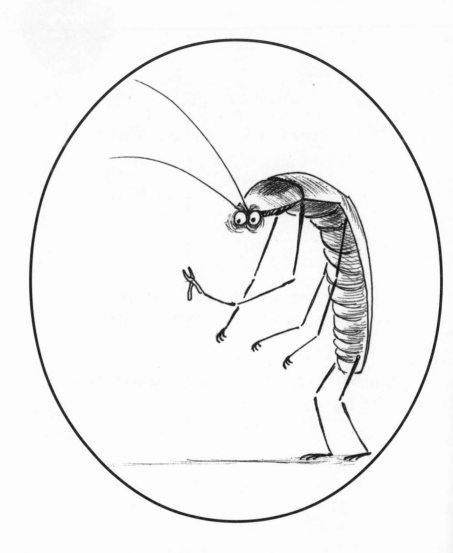

The Roach Clip Rule.

After the joint has burned two thirds of the way, put your roach clip on it. This ensures your enjoyment of the entire joint.

NOTE: *The person smart enough to realize they have reached this point and corrects the situation with proper clip placement gets an extra toke.*

ANOTHER NOTE: *You should be smart enough to complete this task without us telling you how. But, in case you are a total nimrod, here are some instructions:* You should place the clip in such a position, pinching the joint just enough to hold it steady, while still allowing for free passage of the inhaled smoke. You lose a hit if the next person can't take a smooth toke due to improper placement.

The Wasting Paper Rule.

Sometimes rolling papers are hard to come by, so if you waste one intentionally, you are an asshole *(not to be confused with rule #42).*

Your penalty will be that you aren't allowed to smoke any of the joint. You might be allowed to smoke some of the next one, depending on how well your friends like you, and the availability of papers.

If you have just wasted the last paper, you are a total asshole and have to go and buy more papers *(see rule #2).*

NOTE: *Sometimes you tear a paper accidentally. If this happens, you are allowed one more paper to re-roll the joint* (see rule #13). *Unless, of course, you accidentally tore the last paper* (see Rule #60).

The Last Hooter Rule.

It's the last joint, there's no more stash, so you'd better smoke while you can because once it's gone, it's gone!

NOTE: *The last hooter can be any size. It may be small due to the fact that it's the last of the stash. In this instance, pinners are acceptable.*

Glossary

A-Bomb—a combination of drugs, typically marijuana plus opium and heroin. Simon sez: bad vibes!

Acapulco Gold—named after its golden brown color, also called Gold and Gold Leaf. A type of marijuana considered especially potent, grown near Acapulco, Mexico.

Ace—name derives from the highest card in a deck, circa 1940s, an obsolete term describing a marijuana cigarette.

Afkansastan—Afghanistani pot grown in Kansas. Simon sez: this is great pot! See also marijuana.

Alley Cat—A cool record store at 717 Massachusetts in Lawrence, KS.

Anywhere—possessing stash, as in "are you anywhere?" Commonly taken to mean "Do you have any weed?"

Authority Figure(s)—Anyone who can prosecute and/or incarcerate you for smoking (i.e. police, g-men, parents, grandparents, employers, customers, etc.)

African Woodbine—Marijuana cigarette.

Baby—Marijuana cigarette, circa 1940s.

Bag—A predetermined amount of stash that you are purchasing from your connection. Typically referred to as nickel, dime, or quarter bags.

Baked—Very stoned.

Bale—A large quantity of pot, varying in sizes and compressed with wire or twine. Simon sez: Save the bales!

Bambu—Simon's favorite rolling paper.

Bent—From the idea that the mind is warped, altered, high, or intoxicated.

Big Fat—Not to be confused with BIG FAT ONE, it is a large marijuana cigarette smoked to induce lots of euphoria and is also a great tune by Fats Domino and Canned Heat.

Big Fat One—A large marijuana cigarette, smoked to induce lots of euphoria.

Blast—To smoke marijuana as in "I blasted some weed." (circa 1940s) Also used as in BLASTED, to be very high.

Blast Party—A group gathered to smoke marijuana.

Blitzed—Very high.

Blow One—To smoke a joint or marijuana cigarette.

Blow Stick—To smoke a joint.

Bob—Marijuana.

Bogart—The act of taking too long a toke or too many tokes. A person who takes too many tokes or too long of a toke. Ex: That Bogart bummed our stash like a pig with iron lungs.

Bomb/Bomber—A very fat marijuana cigarette. Also used as BOMBED OUT to describe the effect of smoking the same.

Bone—Marijuana cigarettes smoked to induce euphoria.

Bong—A type of pipe used to smoke pot, usually with water acting as filtration and a carburetor to trap the smoke until it is ready to be inhaled. These come in many shapes and sizes.

Bongers—Smoking marijuana using a bong. Doing bong hit and bong hit. Ex: Let's do some bongers!

Brick—A large chunk of compressed marijuana usually weighed in kilograms or pounds.

Buds—The aromatic dried flower tips of the hemp plant. Or, used to refer to all dried flowers and leaves of the hemp plant and smoked to induce euphoria.

Bummer—Getting busted, losing stash, having stash stolen, shitty pot, or simply not having any.

Bummin'—The act of trying to get a joint without paying for it. Or, the feeling that occurs when you don't have any stash.

Bunkweed—Poor or no-quality weed (also known as shitpot, bogus, garbage, trash, you get the idea).

Burn One—Used to describe smoking a joint. Ex: Let's burn one.

Burn/Burned—Getting ripped, stoned, or high. Also used to describe having your stash stolen.

Bush—Marijuana.

Busted—Incarcerated. Simon sez: More bad vibes!

Buzzed—In a very euphoric state from smoking marijuana.

Canadian Black—Named for its color, a variety of marijuana grown in Canada.

Cannabis—The botanical family name of the marijuana plant.

Carburetor—The second air passage located on a bong to act as a siphon to trap smoke in the bong until it is ready to be inhaled. Or, a hole in a joint that passes Rule #8.

Carrying—Possessing marijuana.

Charas—Indian for cannabis.

Cheeba—Another word for cannabis, of unknown origin.

Chillum—A clay pipe with a straight stem issuing from the bottom of the bowl, used in India to smoke pot.

Chitari—Cannabis.

Clean—Not having any stash. Or, to remove all seeds and stems from stash.

Come Down—To experience the end of intoxification.

Connection—The individual(s) you can contact in order to purchase some stash. Also called a CONTACT.

Contact High—The mild high obtained by breathing secondary pot smoke.

Contraband—Any item associated or used with stash. This includes, but is not limited to, bongs, pipes, roachclips, papers etc. Also defined as goods prohibited in trade, or smuggled goods.

Corky's—A cool record store at 5732 Johnson Drive, Shawnee Mission, KS.

Crash—Falling asleep after being high or stoned.

Crutch—see **ROACHCLIP.**

Dagga—Cannabis in South Africa and Jamaica.

Dime—An outdated term used to describe an amount of stash being purchased for $10.

Ditchweed—Garbage pot, shit.

Diamba—Cannabis in Brazil. Also spelled DJAMBA or DJOMA.

Doobie—Another term for a joint. Also spelled DUBY.

'Ere—What is often said when passing a joint from one person to another.

Eighth—A unit of measurement, as in 1/8 of an ounce (or 3.5 grams).

Elbow—448 grams of marijuana.

Enchaioui—From the Arabic, meaning a man who has centered his life around KIF or KEEF (cannabis).

Fatty—A large joint smoked to induce lots of euphoria.

Fire—Matches, lighter, spark, etc.

Fire Up—The act of lighting a joint.

Floating—Another descriptive term for high. Also referred to as FLYING.

Gainesville Green—Very high quality marijuana.

Ganja—High quality marijuana.

Gangster—Marijuana (American slang circa 1940).

Gauge—Marijuana cigarette or joint (American slang circa 1930).

Getting on—Smoking pot (American slang circa 1960).

Giggle Weed—Marijuana, or another name for the hemp plant. A variation of giggle-water, champagne (American slang circa 1910).

Gold—High quality marijuana.

Gold Leaf—Another word for marijuana. See also
  ACAPULCO GOLD.

Golfa—Pot (Mexican slang).

Grass—Cannabis Indica, marijuana (American slang circa 1965). The term was virtually unheard of in England in 1964, but by 1971 the (London) Evening News used the term in reporting on the case of a 14 year old pusher (dealer).

Grasshopper—A pot smoker.

Grass Stains—Describes the green discoloration left on the fingers of a joint roller when they have used an excessive amount of marijuana while rolling the joint.

Green or Green Bud—Another name for the hemp plant.

Grefa—Pot. Also called GRETA, GRIFA, and GRIFFO (Mexican slang).

Gunja—Also called GANGA or GANJA. Common parlance for marijuana amount users of the 1920s (Anglo-Indian slang). By the 1970s, the term (particularly in the second spelling) came to be associated with West Indians (particularly Jamaicans).

Half—A predetermined amount of stash which is being purchased, as in "half ounce" or "half pound." A half ounce is 14 grams, a half pound is 224 grams.

Happy Grass—Marijuana. Also HAY, HEAD.

Head—**1.** Connotes a long-term prison admired by fellow convicts (American slang circa 1942). **2.** A girl or young woman; beatnicks (American slang circa 1950s and 1960s). **3.** A habitual drug user, as in "acid-head," "hop-head," "hemp-head" (American slang circa late 1960s). Possibly derived from the earlier "piss-head" (habitual heavy drinker). **4.** The mind or brain, as in "getting (one's) head together," to concentrate thought; "out of (one's) head," to describe the loss of capacity do to pot (or other drug) use. **5.** A cool movie by the popular music group The Monkees.

Hemp—The whole cannabis plant, including the fibrous stems and roots, in addition to the leaves containing tetrahydrocannabinol (THC), the intoxicating agent of marijuana.

Herb or Herbals—Marijuana (American slang).

Hit—**1.** An assassination, particularly commissioned or executed by gangsters. **2.** The dosage of any particular drug. **3.** The act of inhaling marijuana smoke into your lungs; adopt in Great Britain to also describe sniffing glue.

Hog Leg—Unusually large marijuana cigarette (American slang circa 1960).

Hooter—**1.** A Marijuana cigarette (American slang circa 1970). **2.** A wooden trumpet designed to make a horrible noise (American slang circa 1930). **3.** Breast; adopted as the name of a chain restaurant in the United States.

Indian Hemp or Indian Hay—Cannabis.

Indica—Very high quality marijuana.

Joint—**1.** The most common synonym for "reefer" (American slang circa 1968). Also called JAY, J-SMOKE, JIVESTICK, KICKSTICK, MIGGLE (pl. MUGGLES), MOOCAH (Mexican slang circa 1920), MOOTA, MOOTER, MOOTIE, and MUTAH. **2.** A tent, stall, or any stand from which a grafter provides amusement (American slang circa 1800).

Key—Slang for kilogram; 2.2 pounds of marijuana (or cocaine).

Kickstick—Marijuana cigarette. See also JOINT.

Kill(er) Bud—Great pot.

Kief—Cannabis (North African slang).

Kilo—Short for kilogram; 2.2 pounds.

Kilter—Cannabis or marijuana. See **HEMP.**

Kind-Bud—Great pot.

LB (pound)—Unit of measurement; 448 grams or 16 ounces.

Liamba or Lianda—Cannabis (African slang).

Lid—Obsolete purchasing term used to describe an amount of marijuana (approximately 1 ounce) which had a legendary price of $15 (US); as in a "three finger bag" (American slang circa early 20th century).

Lightweight—Someone who cannot keep up with the group in terms of the amount of marijuana consumed.

Loaded—**1.** In a euphoric state due to pot smoking. **2.** tipsy (American slang circa 1958, particularly among beatniks). **3.** Full of drugs. **4.** Well off, having access to money.

Locoweed—Marijuana (American slang circa 1930).

Loveweed—Marijuana.

Macon—Cannabis (West Africa). Also MACONHA (Brazil).

Mari—Marijuana cigarettes (circa 1920).

Marijuana—**1.** The hemp plant. **2.** The dried flowers and leaves of this plant, especially when smoked to induce euphoria. **3.** The ancient plant of mythological origin which contains the active psychoactive chemical THC.

4. A prohibited plant which has been studied for its purported revolutionary ecological and medicinal uses in the industrialized world. Other names include: ACAPULCO GOLD, AFKANSASTAN, BOB, BUD, CANADIAN BLACK, CANNABIS, CHEEBA, DAGGA, DIAMBA, GANJA, GIGGLE WEED, GREFA, HAPPY GRASS, HAY, HEMP, HERB, HOLY WEED, INDICA, INTSAGA, KIEF/KIF, LIAMBA, LOCOWEED, LOVEWEED, MACON, MACONHA, MARI, ARJI, MARY, MARY ANN, MARY ELLEN, MARY JANE, MARY WARNER, MARY WEAVER, MEXICAN, MEXICAN RED (also PANAMA RED), MOOCAH, MOFA, MOOTA, MOOTER, MOOTIE, MOROCCO GOLD, MUTA, MYAKKA GOLD, REEFER, ROSE MARIE, ROPE, SENSIMILLA, SHIT/SHITPOT, SKUNK BUD, SMOKE, STASH, SWEET LUCY/LEAF, TEA, TRASH, WEED, AND YERBA.

Marijuana Martini—Made from blowing marijuana smoke into a frosted glass or mug; as the smoke lingers in the mug, the glass is slowly tipped, as if to take a drink, and inhaled.

Miggle/Muggles—see **JOINT.**

Myakka Gold—see **MARIJUANA**

Myakka Pinner—Large marijuana cigarettes.

Nickel—An outdated term used to describe an amount of stash being purchased, approximately $5.00 worth.

Number—See **JOINT**

Ounce—28 grams.

Panama Gold/Red—A legendary variety of marijuana of outstanding quality that was grown and smuggled in from South American; particularly known for its distinctive colorful flower buds.

Pinners/Pin Joint—Joints rolled with a small amount of stash.

Pipe—A tube of wood, clay or metal with a mouthpiece at one end and a small bowl at the other end, used for smoking.

Poke—Inhaling a puff of a marijuana cigarette.

Pot—Most common nickname for marijuana.

Pothead—A habitual pot smoker.

Pot-party—A gathering of people smoking marijuana.

Pottsville—Mystical location describing a perception and/or consciousness arrived at through the use of pot or marijuana. Similar to utopia, nirvana or xanadu.

Power Hitter—An accessory item use to smoke a joint without losing any of the smoke.

Quarter—A predetermined amount of stash being purchased (e.g. a quarter-ounce or a quarter-pound).

Q.P.—An abbreviation for a quarter-pound.

Rainy Day Woman—Slang for a joint.

Reefer—See **MARIJUANA.**

Righteous Bush—High quality cannabis (American slang circa 1946). Not to be confused with a former United States President who initiated mass incarcerations of marijuana smokers with unpopular mandatory minimum sentencing policies for judges as a result of the "War on Drugs" (circa 1988-1992).

Ripped—Extremely intoxicated; very stoned.

Roach—**1.** The end of a joint, unofficially defined as the point at which the joint is too short to hold without burning your fingertips. **2.** A nasty bug which is worse in Florida than anywhere else.

Roach Clip—An accessory used to hold the end of a joint in order to be able to continue smoking it without burning fingertips.

Rolling machine—An accessory which purports to roll a perfect joint, but which actually produces an inferior quality marijuana cigarette.

Rolling paper—A paper used to roll marijuana in, in order to smoke it. Often make from a type of rice paper, they are available in a variety of sizes, flavors, patterns, colors, and some come with a wire roach clip built into them.

Root—See **JOINT**

Rope—See **MARIJUANA**

Rose Marie—See **MARIJUANA** (Mexican slang)

Sassafras—See **JOINT** (American slang circa 1944).

Score—To purchase marijuana.

Seeds—**1.** Annoying leftovers from the stash cleaning process. **2.** Precious gifts from God used to grow marijuana.

Sensimilla—Very high quality marijuana.

Shit/Shitpot—Garbage stash that will barely get a fly high.

Shiva/Siva—The Mahedvi, or god, of Hindu mythology who brought marijuana to mankind.

Shlook—See **TOKE.**

Shotgun—Placing the lit end of a joint in your mouth in order to blow the smoke into someone else's mouth. Can be dangerous when the joint is small. Or, the hole made in a pipe chamber to speed smoke through the pipe.

Skin—A rolling paper.

Skunk/Skunk Bud—Aromatic, high quality marijuana.

Smoke—Slang for marijuana.

Smoking Stone—Ceramic or quartz stone hollowed out which is used as a roach clip.

Snop—A marijuana cigarette.

Spaced—As in "spaced out." Describes the euphoric state which results from smoking marijuana.

"Spark It Up!"—To light a joint.

Spleef/Spliff—See **JOINT.**

Stash—See **MARIJUANA.**

Stems—Annoying leftovers from the stash cleaning process.

Stoned—Intoxicated, particularly as a result of smoking marijuana (American and British slang circa 1950s).

Supplier—The person you can contact in order to get stash.

Tea—See **MARIJUANA.**

Tea Party—A gathering where marijuana is smoked.

THC—Tetrahyrdocannabinol, the psychoactive chemical in marijuana.

Thumb—A fat joint.

"Tighten Somebody's Wig"—Give someone marijuana to smoke (American slang circa 1946).

Toke—To inhale from a joint.

Toothpick—A small marijuana cigarette.

Trash—**1.** Garbage. **2.** Stems and seeds left over after cleaning stash. **3.** Low quality marijuana. See also **GARBAGE WEED, SHITPOT**, and **BUNKWEED.**

Trashed—In a euphoric state from smoking marijuana.

Tray—The object on which to clean stash and roll joints.

Viper—A pot smoker.

Wake-n-Bake—The first joint of the day. See also **MORNING HOOTER.**

Wasted—See **TRASHED**

Weed—See **MARIJUANA.**

Yerba—Marijuana.

Z—28 grams of marijuana.

Zig Zag—A brand of rolling papers.

Zoned/Zoned Out—Being high from smoking pot.